Cybersecurity:
Being Cyber Aware
and Cyber Safe

Mini-Book Strategy Series – Book 2

Rand Morimoto, Ph.D.

DEDICATION

I dedicate this book to my children Kelly, Noble, Chip, and Eduardo, for whom we can strive to build a safer world!

ACKNOWLEDGEMENT

I'd like to thank Noble Henderson, who contributed many of the photos found in this book, as well as the consultants at Convergent Computing (CCO), who lend their expertise in providing cybersecurity protection to organizations on a daily basis!

CONTENTS

1 SEEING THE FUTURE FROM THE PRESENT DAY

Present day cyberattacks are just a snapshot of our future. From credit cards stolen from retailers and online stores, to cyber espionage, to financial system breeches, we see more and more incidents occurring, and we're just scratching the surface what will be in our future. Individuals, eCommerce hosters, and enterprises need to step up their cybersecurity protection efforts at a time when users on various endpoint devices are wanting more and easier access to information. It's a challenge that needs to be and will be addressed over the upcoming years.

Cyber Data Access from Anywhere

Back during the days of the wild wild west, the only way to rob someone or to rob a bank was to confront someone face to face with a weapon and ask them for their money. With Cybercrimes, the victim is rarely confronted directly, and the criminal can effectively rob thousands or millions of individuals from the comfort of their home.

In recent credit card thefts, the criminal is thousands of miles away, accesses databases of poorly protected retail and online systems, and collects data to be sold and used to acquire cash and make credit card purchases. The criminal never has to face his victims in person, and with such great distances from the criminal to the crime, the impersonal nature of the crime makes it the near perfect crime.

Many face to face robbers "chicken out" at the last minute when they are confronted in person with their victim. Bank robbers who are simply told "no" by a teller have been known to just turn around and leave the bank, despite the threat of "having a gun". Other criminals fear physical retribution from their victim, and thus talk themselves out of committing a crime.

But cybercriminals can access data, online cash, online resources from anywhere, making the source point of crimes being any of millions of internet connection points from around the globe.

Cyber Espionage to Access Trade Secrets

Besides financial crimes of credit card theft and online financial system thefts, cyber espionage now pits businesses against other businesses, governments against other governments. No longer does a spy need to train and be groomed for decades to be able to physically infiltrate an organization when someone with sophisticated cybersecurity capabilities access trade secrets from anywhere.

And with the growth of cloud computing, cyberspies don't even need to break their way into hardened corporate and government networks when trade secrets are inadvertently stored in publicly accessible file sharing systems on the Web. The convenience of access to technology has advanced faster than security policies and practices, as such, users walking around with unsecured mobile devices synchronizes or backup data to cloud-based services not realizing the vast distribution of confidential and protected data they are spreading to potentially unprotected and definitely unmanaged storage destinations.

Why should a spy spend years preparing to break into an office to steal data files when the person can simply snatch a tablet device left sitting on a table as an individual walks up to get a new cup of coffee at a Starbucks? Or from a digital perspective, the spy can work from home in another country and access unencrypted content stored in cloud-based file sharing systems. Espionage has gotten simple now that data is openly stored in online and unprotected mobile devices.

Cyber Technology Used for Old Fashion Physical Crimes

Cybercrimes can take place converting digital knowledge into cold hard cash. In a 2013 ATM heist, overseas criminals were able to raise withdrawal limits on user accounts and then walk to ATM machines to withdraw cash from ATM machines in a night. The effort was well coordinated with dozens of individuals simultaneously withdrawing cash from hundreds of

ATM machines, netting the crime scheme perpetrators with millions of dollars[i].

Cyber technologies are used in conjunction with physical devices to create a new vector for crime that blended the digital era with physical cash systems.

Converting Digital Cash into Physical Goods

Other methods of converting digital cash into physical goods are frequently done where cybercriminals go online and make an online purchase, have goods delivered to an address (home or apartment), and the criminal walks up to the delivery point and takes the goods off the doorstep. Online retailers have made it simple for shoppers to simply do a "1-click" purchase where their credit card number and shipping information is in a system so that a cyber-thief simply needs to know the person's logon and password to their online retail account.

Because many recipients of goods are not home when goods are placed on their doorstep, the cybercriminal just shows up to the delivery address and picks up the goods off the doorstep and walks away. These petty crimes happen daily with consumer electronic goods or household items, however the same is done with Corporate purchase accounts on large construction shipments of copper wire, marble tiles, and brass pipe fittings delivered to shipping dock for signature of receipt. Large scale "cargo thief" of entire shipping containers full of goods go missing or are acquired using fake credentials[ii].

Cyber Defamation and Cyber Bullying

Cybercrimes extend beyond direct financial models for gain, to areas of cyber defamation and cyber bullying. Instead of gaining from cyber activities, another angle is to attack a competitor or individual to decrease their presence and thus improve that of oneself

Defamation of an individual or a business may be done for spiteful reasons, because of hatred of the individual, or it could simply be a defacing of another business Website to prevent customers from visiting, or buying goods and services from a competitor.

Cyber bullying is commonly referenced to teenagers making fun of others through social media, posting compromising pictures, things that are just the digital version of playground taunting. These are no doubt very painful and hurtful to the victim, and the widespread nature of the internet means that the impact can reach far beyond a handful of individuals on the playground, but to friends, peer groups, even to individuals the victim doesn't know yet but may encounter at some time in the future.

But cyber defamation and cyber bullying can have far reaching impact as the victim may retaliate from a cyber-taunt with a guns and weapons to kill dozens of people the person knows and many times people the person doesn't know. Business cyber defamation can cause a business to unnecessarily go out of business, creating unemployment for workers and could cause a good business that provides valuable services to a community to no longer exist.

Cybercrimes do not necessarily need to involve the direct loss of cash or credit information, but could hurt individuals and communities, impacting hundreds if not thousands of downstream vendors, employees, and consumers.

Cyber Zombies

Cybercrimes also do not always have to take place between individuals or in real time. Cybersecurity attacks can be initiated by the installation of malicious code on systems of unsuspecting victims, and at some point in time, the code is activated and a coordinated attack is initiated.

The zombies could be used to block legitimate access to a Website by having the zombies send thousands of invalid requests to the site, thus prevent legitimate access. Zombies could be used to maliciously run code on distributed systems to delete content, capture logons and passwords, install or uninstall software, or the like. Bots (digital robots) and cybercrimes are on a rise, and organizations need to protect themselves from this form of digital attack[iii].

The zombie code is activated to do some type of activity at some point in time, and the actions could impact individual systems (but thousands of them) or the actions could target the attack on a destination target.

Summary

Cybercrimes take various shapes and forms, from direct attacks on financial systems, indirect attacks on financial systems utilizing technology to control ATM machine networks, even cyber espionage and cyber-defamation, bullying, and zombies. But the biggest concern about cybercrimes is they can be conducted at any time, from anywhere, and impact thousands if not millions of victims at the same time.[iv]

We have only begun to see the start of serious cybercrimes, and it is the role and responsibility of individuals, businesses, government agencies, eCommerce hosted providers, and effectively "everyone" who leverages the Internet to simplify how the individual conducts business and interacts with others.

This book focuses on the awareness of cybersecurity threats, and what individuals and organizations need to do to do their part in the cyber-protection of users and digital assets.

2 EARLY DAY VIRUSES AND WORMS WERE CHILD'S PLAY

As much as computer viruses and computer threats existed back during the days of floppy disk based systems with "boot sector viruses" and the like, it really wasn't until the dawn of the public Internet that cybersecurity threats became more common place. That's because the mere fact of connecting a computer to the Internet created an open gateway between the computer system and the vast unknown. And in the early days of the Internet, most users were using the Internet for basic email exchange, which is why the first security threats came in the form of email viruses.

Wake Up Call that Computer Systems Were Insecure

It was some of the early computer viruses that started to show up in enterprise, things like the Chernobyl Virus (1998), Melissa Virus (1999),

LoveBug (2000), and Code Red / Nimda worm (2001) that started to change security processes in the corporate world and world of government, education, and for home users. These viruses and worms were being attached to email messages or within documents that users share across the Internet that would then spread within a home or business.

Anti-virus software was around for years, but through lax implementation, many organizations either didn't have anti-virus software completely implemented on all systems in the enterprise, or while the anti-virus software was installed, there was no mechanism to keep the software up to date. Viruses were popping up weekly, and unless a system was regularly updated, systems would be exposed.

Organizations began to realize that there was more than a need to image and deploy systems, but to make sure the systems were kept up to date so that the systems would be protected against evolving security threats again them.

Hobbyists Seeking their 15-Minutes of Fame

Early cybersecurity threats were for the most part being created and propagated by hobbyist seeking their 15-minutes of fame[v]. Most were simply trying to prove they could create a virus, and potentially end up on the 6pm nightly news as the creator of a virus "sweeping the globe."

Simon Vallor, a Web designer from North Wales was caught after boasting about creating a series of viruses in a chatroom. When caught, he said he didn't expect the viruses to create any harm, and was really just trying to see what he could do by creating and spreading the virus[vi].

In one case, a Michael Buen from the Philippines was involved in the creation and distribution of a Word macro virus that would intercept the print command on a system and print a copy of the Mr. Buen's resume. In this particular case, it wasn't difficult for the authorities to track the guy down[vii].

In another early cybersecurity incident, socialite Paris Hilton's phone account was accessed and the data (including phone numbers and photos) were posted on the Internet. Through a basic security attack, the process to change a password on the then T-Mobile Sidekick network was to enter in your favorite pet's name. It was public knowledge that Paris Hilton had a Chihuahua that she admired, and thus it was obvious to the hacker what her favorite pet's name was, and thus her account password was easily changed and accessed[viii].

There are many lessons to have been learned from these early hacker and security attacks, like to NOT use your real favorite pet's name, or to make sure your system is patched and updated with the latest anti-malware software, and to not open a document that you don't know where the content came from. Which sadly even a decade or more later, people still succumb to the basic holes in security.

Fortunately for events that occurred in the 1990s and 2000s, most of the attacks were being done by hobbyists who were merely trying to see what they could do with viruses or computer systems, and how far they can get with their programming skills. Their reach and access was extensive, but in most cases resulted in community service or at most a year or two in jail.

Copycats Spawn Continued Security Impact on Systems

From the early days of virus writing, a single virus may spawn months and years of copycat virus "editors" who take a virus, make a few changes to the virus, and then a new "variant" of the virus is wild on the Internet. The individuals doing these virus edits were frequently called "script kiddies"[ix] referring to amateurs (again) simply editing code and getting their 15-minutes of fame.

One such instance of a copycat virus writer was one Jeffrey Lee Parson, who at age 18 took the well-known Blaster virus, made a few edits to the virus (which was then classified as the Blaster-B Worm variant) that required anti-virus software companies to edit their detection software to "look' for this new variant. In the case of the variant created by Parsons, his version of the worm contained a Trojan horse component that communicated back to a Website Mr. Parson's had created. Again, it didn't take authorities long to track down Mr. Parsons because his tracks were well laid out in the virus[x].

In most cases the copycat viruses and worms were just simple variants, however in time, the copycat viruses were reprogrammed and address weaknesses of the original virus or worm, and thus future releases of the viruses and worms were more destructive. So while much of the viruses and worms were the work of kids or hobbyists, there were some strains of viruses and worms that had great impact on users.

Impact More Disruptive than Catastrophic

The early virus and worm writers and those who created copycat variants for the most part created disruptive tools that opened up a whole industry of anti-virus software companies, security protection tools, and virus clean-up services. The impact was more disruptive than catastrophic, if anything, the writing was on the wall though that the computer industry and anyone with a computer will forever be impacted by threats of security breaches, and organizations as well as users had to create processes and procedures to protect themselves from computer attacks.

Regardless of the impact the virus or worm had, the fact that an attack may have successfully infected a system or any system identified a vulnerability, and users in the industry had to speed up their adoption and ability to address security vulnerabilities faster than the viruses and worms were being released in the wild.

3 EARLY DAY ENTERPRISE RESPONSE

By the late 1990's, enterprises were being hit with virus attack after virus attack, in some cases so debilitating that the organization could not send email messages for a day or two until the virus was cleaned up. In other instances, systems had to be shutdown or rebuilt after a virus or worm made the system unusable. It was clear to enterprises that they had to create methodical processes and procedures to keep ahead of the attackers.

Enterprise Awareness that Patching and Updating was a Necessity

The two major areas that enterprises had to focus on were regular system patches and updates to fix bugs and vulnerabilities in software, and to regularly update anti-virus software to keep up with the regular release of "signature files" that look for the latest viruses and worms along with the copycat viruses and worms that followed. In the mid-1990s, there was little done to regularly patch and update systems. When systems weren't connected to the outside world, it was rare for a system to get infected or at least the rate of infection was controlled by how quickly individuals moved floppy disks between systems to share files. This was a slow process, and early attacks were limited.

But again, with the opening up of the Internet and users getting infected emails, a vulnerability in an operating system or application was easier to exploit, and the organization had to make sure their operating system and applications were updated. As an example, early viruses compromised a Microsoft Word "macro" function that allowed users to create and run macros, back in the day to create things like headers, salutations, create common document formats, and the like.[xi] But a compromise to the macro system allowed a virus to automatically delete files, or create files that were not desired by the owner of the system. Microsoft released a patch to Microsoft Word that disabled the automatic macro feature, which today in the latest versions of Microsoft Word, you specifically are warned and notified that a macro is embedded in a file, and by default the macro is disabled so you have to specifically enable the macro to run it or resave the file.

But in the early days, the Microsoft update with the default macro behavior change came in a patch that had to be installed, however if a system was not patched or updated, the vulnerability still existed. For an unpatched and un-updated system, the user was dependent on their anti-virus software to capture the file attachment with the malicious code. All it takes is a copycat script kiddie to write a variant and push a variant out before the anti-virus software vendors could update their anti-virus signature files for the virus to impact a system. Thus it was important to not only have an anti-virus software installed, but also the core operating system and applications patched and updated.

Patches and Updates Needed Better Coordination

Early on, software vendors were releasing patches and updates to systems as soon as the updates became available, so enterprise were constantly rushing to install new updates when the updates were released, sometimes on a Tuesday morning, sometimes on a Wednesday afternoon, something on a Saturday evening.

By the fall of 2003, Microsoft helped the marketplace by changing their updates to be released on the second Tuesday of every month[xii]. This standard cadence GREATLY assisted organizations around the world as they were now able to plan for the monthly round of updates from Microsoft, test the updates, and roll them out with some coordination.

This monthly update cycle was quickly adopted by many other vendors, and as such, the concept of a "monthly maintenance window" was included as a best practice for organizations as they released updates on a more methodical manner.

Year 2000 (Y2K) Forced a Global Awareness for the Need of Systems Management

While the initial outbreak of viruses and worms started to have organizations take note of a need to centrally manage and administer patches and updates, the Year 2000 rolled along where systems had to be checked, patched, and updated to make sure they recognized the year 2000 as 2000, and not as 1900 or some other year. Most modern systems were properly prepared to acknowledge the pending change in the millennium, however a combination of old systems and applications AND the uncertainty of other systems caused a flurry of manual checks and tests.

If systems were interconnected and centrally managed, a check of systems and applications could have been deployed to validate system readiness. So network administrators, after the outbreak of viruses and worms, along with a mad dash to address Y2K made it very clear to enterprises that if they didn't have a systems management system in place, that they dearly needed one.

Daylight Savings Time (DST) Update Reinforced the Necessity for System Management

Right after everyone took a deep breath that Y2K was behind them, a new event popped up which was the change to the dates that Daylight Savings Time was to take place in the United States. The United States Congress voted to adopt the Energy Policy Act of 2005 where daylight savings time would be extended in an effort to decrease the energy consumption of the nation.

This change was intended to adjust the dates of daylight savings time to better match patterns of commutes in a post-agrarian America when daylight savings time was originally established. The United States no longer had the focus of its workforce tending to harvests, and instead was an office and factory-based workforce. While the impact of daylight savings time was to benefit the new workforce, the simple change of when computer clocks and software were to "spring forward" and "fall back" created a significant problem for anyone with a device with a daylight savings time aware clock, like a personal computer system.[xiii]

Systems that were expected to Fall back on a specific date had to be adjusted so that they fell back on a different date. Calendar appointments scheduled for specific times of the day had to address the change in the time variation. Even with the best laid plans, for a several month period, clocks, calendars, meeting appointments, and systems failed to work as expected. DST resulted in more problems than Y2K.

After DST, it was very clear to organizations that centralized management and administration was needed, and by the 2008, most organizations finally had some form of automated patching, updating, and centralized management system in their enterprise, which in turned helped the organization be better able to address security threats as they arose.

4 SHIFT FROM HOBBYIST HACKERS TO PROFESSIONALS

From early day hackers, to enterprises focused on centralized management and administration, the period from 1995-2005 was one where organizations truly developed enterprise focused policies and processes. It was timely for these organizations to be prepared as the mid-2000's saw a clear shift of security threats transferring from hobbyists to professionals.

Stock Manipulation and Online Theft Started to Take Hold

In 2007, Nordea Bank in Sweden was hacked and over a 15-month period, a $1-million was stolen using a Trojan horse virus that captured the logon and account access information of about 250 bank customers accessing their accounts online. The hackers got away with the scheme for a longer period of time because they transferred very small amounts over a long period of time, thus avoiding detection by automated transaction validation systems. At the time, this attack was the "biggest hack ever,"[xiv] although it was only a matter of time that security attacks would have even greater impact on consumers and enterprises.

In 2008, there were a couple high visibility stock manipulation incidents where a hacker from India (Thirugnanam Ramanathan) performed what is called a "hack, pump, and dump" scheme where stocks are electronically manipulated through a hack attack, prices rise, and the hacker then dumps the stock for a profit.[xv] In a separate incident a hacker from the Ukraine (Oleksandr Dorozhko) hacked into a computer to gather advance information about a negative earnings announcement, and used the information to net himself a profit of over $250,000 over a 6-day period.[xvi]

These and many other incidents in the mid-2000's clearly marked a shift of hack attacks beyond the work of hobbyists to individuals (and professionals) that were clearly after a significant financial gain from their efforts.

Organized Crime Syndicates Shifts to Cybercrimes

By 2009, the FBI was identifying over 50% of the cybersecurity breaches were being performed by organized crime syndicates. It was much easier for the organized crime perpetrators to commit crimes electronically than to steal money the old fashion way.

The Internet provided a means of access that extended far beyond the traditional border and territory of the crime syndicate, and the perpetrators never had to leave their homes or face risk of capture on their home soil.

Beyond the profile of the attacker being from organized crime, the purpose of attack extended from being an immediate access to information, to one where information is gathered, and then used at a future date to coordinate the compromise of systems.

This profile change in the organized and professional manner in which cybercrimes were taking place created a whole new challenge for law enforcement agencies at the time, and it required a coordinated effort to work through a resolution to the problem.

Global Jurisdictions Hamper Global Law Enforcement

One of the challenges law enforcement had in dealing with hack attacks was the lack of global cooperation in tracking down and punishing cybercriminals. For an individual in one country hacking systems in another country, the target country being attacked had to go to the source country to apprehend the criminal. However the source country where the hacker resided had limited motivation to go after the perpetrator because no crime on their soil was being conducted.

Even if the source country law enforcement rounded up the individual, the laws of the country did not address "hack attacks performed against individuals and businesses in another country". It took a while before cybersecurity was an issue for every country to address, and that law enforcement in various countries took responsibility to assist in apprehending criminals and extraditing them to face their crimes.

This process of developing global jurisdictions took a better part of 2005 through 2011/2012 before a more coordinated effort was adhered to on a global basis.

Domestic Law Enforcement Limited by Jurisdiction

However the problem of law enforcement wasn't just a global issue, even cities, counties, and states in the United States had challenges with jurisdiction. A local police department has no jurisdiction to pursue crimes created in other cities or for that matter outside of the country. Even crimes that span U.S. state borders required law enforcement of each state to coordinated efforts to pursue perpetrators across borders.[xvii]

One of the first things that local law enforcement agencies needed was training. Most officers in the late 1990s and early 2000s had no training on cyber law enforcement. With knowledge on how to address cybercrimes, existing laws and enforcement processes were able to be used to expand jurisdictions to address the new wave of crimes being conducted globally.

Decline in Identity Theft Gives Way to Simpler Crimes by Numbers

By 2010, identity theft of individual accounts was on the decline due to better security controls by banks and institutions in minimizing the impact to consumers. However cybercriminals have become tech savvy and have developed better methods of stealing more money in a shorter amount of time.[xviii] Today's cybercriminals attack large institutions and gain millions of credit card numbers and user logons and passwords than the efforts of the past decade where a cybercriminal was impersonating one individual at a time.

Identity theft was too difficult to perform relative to other options in mass identity compromise, as such, a shift in focus for law enforcement agents and forensic experts to focus on large risks targeted events.[xix]

5 WHAT IS BEING DONE TO HELP PROTECT YOU

With all of the cybercriminals around us and what seems to be a relatively easy access to information by the criminals, the question that is often asked is "what is being done to protect me?" As was noted in the last chapter, law enforcement training as well as the issue with jurisdiction needed to be addressed. It was a slow process to get laws, regulations, and law enforcement ready to address this new wave of crimes, however all things considering, the decade of time it took to get things relatively well addressed was quite quick.

Case Law Creating Legal Precedence for Jurisdiction

To be able to address security breaches, law enforcement agencies needed to be able to apply laws to the crimes being conducted. Cybercrimes were not even of focus prior to the 1990s, as such, legal precedence needed to be created applying other laws in the books to the cybercrimes.

The early cases set this precedence, and one of the main laws used to pursue cybercriminals was that of trespassing.[xx] A cybercriminal accessing a computer system that does not belong to them, and is not under their control or management was identified as trespassing. As such, a cybercriminal could be held and their personal systems seized as instruments of trespassing.

Once trespassing was used to hold cybercriminals, other existing laws were used to pursue an individual including theft, stock manipulation, credit card fraud, or the like. The key was to hold individuals for an initial crime long enough to use forensic techniques to identify other crimes an individual has conducted.

Laws and Regulations Caught up with Technology

Along with evolving laws were the enactment of regulations that "encouraged" businesses to be more proactive in their roles in cybersecurity protections.

One such regulation was enacted by the credit card industry called the Payment Card Industry (PCI) data security standard. After a number of credit card thefts off websites due to lax security practices, the credit card companies required retailers accepting credit cards to ensure their computer networks were secure, to require encryption of information, restrict access of cardholder data, and enable the ability to track and monitor access controls.

Failure to meet these requirements meant a retailer would not be able to accept credit cards, which for most businesses would mean the end of the business in its ability to accept a common form of payment.

Other laws such as the Health Insurance Portability and Accountability Act (HIPAA) as well as local laws like the State of California Social Security Number Confidential law (CCC 1798.85), Shredding Law (CCC 1790.80-82), and Credit Card Truncation Law (CCC 1747.9) were enacted to eliminate personally identifiable information like social security numbers, home address, date of birth, and credit card information from being easily stored, accessed, and compromised.

Police Departments Getting Cyber Savvy

As noted in the previous chapter, it was important for local law enforcement agencies to come up to speed on cybercrimes, including training as well as having tools and resources available to them to pursue cybercriminals and bring them to justice.

Law enforcement agencies in the Silicon Valley of the San Francisco Bay Area were some of the first in the nation that led the way in officer training to identify cybercrimes, perform forensics, and pursue the criminals.[xxi] Task forces were created to address crimes such as unauthorized online access, online child pornography, cyberbullying, intellectual property theft, and cyber-impersonation.

Similar models for law enforcement training, use of tools, and practices have been replicated around the country, providing better and broader experienced law enforcement agents on the street.

Federal Bureau of Investigation Cyber Division

To aid in cybercrimes that expanded beyond the boundaries of a city, county, or state jurisdiction, the Federal Bureau of Investigation (FBI) by mandate of the President of the United States, created the National Cyber Investigative Joint Task Force (NCIJTF) to be the focal point for all government agencies to coordinate, integrate, and share information related to all domestic cyberthreat investigations.[xxii]

The NCIJTF coordinates the cyberthreat investigation between the Central Intelligence Agency (CIA), Department of Defense (DoD), Department of Homeland Security (DHS), the National Security Agency (NSA), FBI field offices, and local law enforcement agencies across the country.

The FBI aid comes in the form of information access, centralized reporting, cross-jurisdictional support, international espionage, or support when the scale of an attack exceeds the capabilities of a local jurisdiction.

Evolution of the Psychology of Cybercrimes

While much of the efforts of cybersecurity protection is technology based, many of the recent efforts have been focused on the psychology of cybercrimes, effectively efforts to think one or two steps ahead of the criminals. Technology-based efforts commonly identify a crime in progress, which is too late. By profiling the attacker and identifying past incidents and efforts, law enforcement agents can seek to identify future actions of the cybercriminal, and seek to catch the individual before a next attack occurs.

Much of the predictive analysis processes use a form of Game Theory, similar to the game of chess, where each participant tries to identify and predict the next step of their opponent. By using forensics to analyze the potential future cybercrime efforts of individuals and organized crime rings, law enforcement efforts can be coordinated to thwart cybercrimes before they impact individuals.

Leveraging Decades Old Motivational Theories to Combat Cybercrimes

A counterpart to the predictive analysis of games theory is the arena of Motivational Systems Theory, or MST, published by Martin Ford in 1992.[xxiii] Ford's theory simplifies the notion that people do the things they do through motivation, and by identifying their motivation, one can gain insight what someone will do next.

So simply identifying the predictive nature of actions, one can postulate a potential outcome, however by adding in motivational factors, the resulting assessment could be more accurately estimated.

When performing an analysis of decision factors as they relate to cybercrimes, the detective and forensic analysts want to leverage whatever they can to narrow down their search and reach an outcome of capturing cybercriminals as promptly as possible.

Expansion of Forensic Techniques in Cyber Analysis

For decades, forensics has been used to narrow down the search criteria and come to a conclusion based on information and analysis. The same forensic practices can be used in the isolation of cybercrime cases. Multipoint variables are used to gather data, trace historical data back, and use predictive and motivational theories to guess forward.

And in the world of Big Data where information from multiple sources can be captured and analyzed, data analysis helps the forensic scientists narrow down on the information they are seeking to assess.

6 WHAT INDIVIDUALS CAN DO TO PROTECT AGAINST CYBERCRIMES

As much as there are laws and regulations set out to help protect businesses and individuals, at the end of the day, everyone has to do their part to keep cyber aware and be cyber safe.

Public Information is Publicly Available

One of the challenges in trying to maintain the privacy of information is that a lot of information is public information, and in this day and age, that public information is available through public database searches. Public information includes things like court records, property tax records, and public filings. These are things you have no control over and can provide a lot information like where you live, what you pay in property taxes, in a case of court records it would include potentially driving information, divorce record information, and the like.

There are tricks that a good divorce attorney, a good criminal law attorney, a good civil law attorney will know how to flag the body content of a court filing as non-public information so that only the first page of a filing is publicly available. However while one can minimize the amount of information shared in public records, there's just some information on all public records that is searchable and publicly available.

Be Mindful of What You Share Online

However there's a LOT of information that individuals can choose to make available or not, and that's up to the individual to decide how much information they want to share. Starting with something as simple as a home phone number having a phone number "listed" or not is one way. But then when one gets into the realm of social media like Facebook, Instagram, Imgur, Twitter, LinkedIn, and the like, this is where users need to be very conscious of the information available.

When information is posted on any social media site, one needs to consider the information freely and publicly available to anyone UNLESS specific steps are taken to limit access to the information. While one would hope that the information is private by default, quite the opposite. The information by most social media providers is public by default, or at least each user needs to assume it is that way and take steps to validate that assumption.

It's okay to post pictures of your dog, kids, and other personal information, but then be aware that can't be used as your "secret words" or "secret phrases". If your dog's name is Fido, and you post pictures of Fido throughout your social media sites, for your secret question, you don't want to answer that your "Name of your favorite pet" is "Fido". Pick something completely different so that it isn't the same or even close, maybe even a best friends favorite pet's name followed with $!## or something that makes it even harder. End of the day, if you make it harder for people to guess the answers to your secret questions, then you increase your security a bit.

Watch Out for Phishing

A common practice that attackers use is to masquerade as legitimate business that potentially the recipient uses (a bank, a credit card company, a department store or online company) and they make the person think they need to logon or provide private information. This "phishing" technique is used to extract credit card information, bank information, passwords and the like from users where the information is then used to access the real sites.

While some users are familiar with these types of incoming messages, it is amazing how users still can be fooled. A recent attack was conducted at a U.S. Airport where a Wi-Fi-hotspot was setup that made travelers believe they were getting access to Free Wi-Fi at the airport. The hotspot took users to a page that noted "this airport has made a special arrangement with over 2,000 businesses to provide free Wi-Fi to their employees. Enter in your company email address to see if your company is participating in this free program." Users would enter in their company email address and then be informed that their company IS participating in the free program, so all they need to do is enter in a password and they will get 2-hours of free Wi-Fi. Amazingly, almost every person who was caught in this phishing attack entered in their normal business password that is typically associated with their email address!

Within 4-hours, the attackers had over 200 corporate email addresses and passwords from some of the most prominent organizations in the world.

A few lessons to learn, to ALWAYS be cautious about something that is free, especially when the systems asks a logon and password. And if you do provide a password to a site you likely will never return to again (like a free Wi-Fi hotspot site), use a password that you NEVER use for normal logon accounts!

Leveraging One-time or Limited Time Payment Mechanisms

For users that buy products over the Internet, that is another vector to acquire and access personal information. When providing a credit card to a site, never use a Debit (bank) card, always use a Visa or MasterCard type credit card. With credit cards, you are typically limited to just US$50 in unauthorized charges, the credit card company assumes the balance of the liability. The key is that you "responsibly" use and store your card. A Debit (bank) card does not have the same limits on liability, as such, a cyber-thief can drain your bank account and it could be days, weeks, months, or never before you'll get your money back.

And even with credit cards, most credit card companies provide a "one-time" card number. Check with your credit card company, but if you pay your credit card online, there's usually an option to get a "one-time card number". It's a 16-digit credit card number that you specify the amount you want to allocate to this number and the expiration, so if you know you'll be making a $250 purchase in the next couple weeks, you can specify a $250-$300 limit and 30-day expiration. A special 16-digit number is issued that can be used for the purchase, and that number is only valid once for the amount noted. It is different from your main credit card number, so if the number is compromised, your main card number is not compromised, nor can anyone charge anything over the limit you note.

Another option is to use credit card "Gift Cards" that you can purchase online or commonly at grocery stores. You can "fill" the cards with whatever limit you want, whether it's $25, $100, $250, and you can make charges to the gift card. If the card# is compromised, you typically still have the $50 maximum credit card liability limit, and it does not impact your normal credit card, credit card credit line, or other credit history. It is important to read the fine print on the various cards, some gift cards have very expensive usage fees where they charge a fee each time the card is used, or the credit balance expires or incurs a monthly fee. There are plenty of cards that will charge as little as a $3.75 fee (or less) once, and the money on the card never expires and no fees are charged thereafter. You don't want to protect yourselves against the cyber-thieves and get "robbed" by the credit card companies from their transaction fees!

Being Mindful of the Content You Access

Also as you are living and working in the world of the online Internet, be aware of attachments, Website links, even content on sites that you visit. "Read" what you are being asked to do, many times even semi-legitimate sites will have various links on the site that look like the right place to click to access the information you were searching for. However, if you spent a fraction of a second to read the button you are about to click, you'll frequently find the button says it'll take you to an advertisement site, or it's sending you to a download site to access content you were not requesting.

On a desktop computer, you can hover over a link and usually see where the link is taking you, where the target destination should be something similar or close to what you are looking to access. If you think you are going to the Bank of America website but the URL is taking you to something not even close to Bank of America, then do NOT click to follow the link. As more and more users use their phone or tablet to access content, where the touch screens don't always make it easy to preview the link where you are going, you need to be even MORE cautious of following a link.

Also, if an attachment or a download is an "executable" file such as an EXE executable file, a script file, or an applicable that wants to "install" something on your system, unless you specifically expected to install something on your system, abort the installation immediately! If you don't know how to abort the installation, turn off your system, be very cautious on installers. We hear on the news all the time how some spyware software, or BOT software is installed on hundreds of systems, and the way these software and BOTs get on systems is because people actually allow them to be installed. The users are knowingly being asked to install something, and they agree.

34

Scan Your System(s) Periodically to Make Sure You Know Everything Installed on Them

Having an anti-malware software on your system will typically identify unauthorized software being installed on your system. However occasionally something might find their way on your system, which is very possible when a system is shared with others. When asked whether a system is shared, most users will say they are the only user of a system, until reminded of that they occasionally will let someone in their family surf the Internet to quickly check an email, share a system while traveling (and the business traveler's system is connected to the hotel/resort Internet and everyone quickly users that system).

A quick scan of installed software on a system such as looking at the Applications folder on a Windows System or on an Apple Mac, or going to the Control Panel under Installed Software (or Add/Remove Programs) and look at the list of software installed on a system. Many times a user might not be completely aware of what some of the software installed on a system really is or does, like on Microsoft Windows Systems, many times things like .NET Framework, or Visual C++, or the like are installed on the systems by (legitimate) business applications. But a quick look of the installed software plus a quick Google search of the name of the application installed will allow a user to better understand whether the software installed is business or legitimate software, or whether it might be malware.

Malware should be removed and immediately uninstalled from the system. If the system is a business system, the organization's Help Desk or nearby technical guru might be of help to identify inappropriate software and can assist with the uninstallation of such software.

Keep Track of your Stuff

Lastly, as much as cybercrimes are typically considered to be "over the Internet crimes" and users are on the look-out for malware in emails, documents, and the like, physical crimes are JUST as dangerous as cybercrimes in getting your information. It is amazing how many times users walk away from their phone, tablet, or laptop in a coffee shop when they get a refill, or they put all their stuff down to save a table and then go place an order and are gone from their systems for 5, 10, 15 minutes without ever looking back to see if someone is observing them watch their stuff.

A cyber-thief can pick-up a system and take off with it, and through an unlocked phone or tablet, gain access to logon accounts and passwords, that can then help the criminal access content on a laptop. Or users who make it convenient by having their systems "remember their password", a person to grabs a system can easily logon without needing to access a password at all.

A cyber-thief may just be interested in getting a list of contacts off one system, to then be able to send phishing emails to someone on the contact list to gain information. A stolen laptop of a Top Executive of an organization that sends an email to all of their direct reports can get a number of employees to send sales information, internal documents, or other information without the recipients even thinking twice. A rise in scams targeting corporate executives to inadvertently give up credential access so that the crime is not directly targeted at the executive, but to impersonate the executive to gather information from subordinates.[xxiv] So it's not just information that might be on the system, but it's the information that person can extract from others.

7 THE ROLES AND RESPONSIBILITIES OF ENTERPRISES IN CYBER PROTECTION

In the last chapter, a number of examples were provided on how individuals can protect themselves or be extra careful about cybercriminals. However enterprises cannot assume that all of their employees are clearly aware of cybersecurity protections, protection against malware, protection against phishing attacks, and employees occasionally need to be reminded to keep track of their "stuff" so that their devices aren't stolen.

Making Sure Employees are Trained and Aware of their Basic Individual Responsibilities

As with anything, people have to be trained and made aware of what they need to know, and security protection is no different. Organizations should conduct organization wide awareness campaigns on security and best practices, and regularly update training and reinforce training practices to employees. For organizations with high turnover, seasonal workers, even organizations that are growing quickly, having a regular routine of training is important to ensure EVERYONE is keeping up with the security and protection message.

It is most effective when the security is driven from the top of the organization, down through the organization so that employees understand this is of great importance to the protection of organizational secrets and intellectual property, which should be of interest to every person in the organization.[xxv]

Training sessions need to be informative and prescriptive, providing direct guidance and real world examples. After 2-3 reminder sessions, users will tune out to the "same message" over and over.[xxvi] However if new security threats, new sample real world attacks are shared, employees will be more apt to listen and apply the learning to their day to day experiences.

Implementing Standard Endpoint and Server Protections

With the user participating in the security and protection process, there are things an organization can do on the "backend" and on the user's device level to provide protection. The reason this is addressed AFTER the user is trained is because if systems are put in place for security and protection, users many times will just relay on what is put in place for them and minimize their role and responsibility. By placing user security at the start, the systematic protections are there to help the user with their level of security.

The systematic security are things like network firewalls, anti-virus and anti-malware tools on all systems, client and server firewalls, and the latest patches and updates recommended by manufacturers installed on all systems and devices. These protections are considered best practices, however again, they by themselves are not going to protect a user or organization from all security threats. As such, security best practices are applied as part of the normal security protection process.

A couple handy guides for endpoint security have been published by the United States Department of Commerce in their National Institute of Standards and Technology (NIST) guides 800-94 "Guide to Intrusion Detection and Prevention Systems"[xxvii], and 800-83 "Guide to Malware Incident Prevention and Handling for Desktops and Laptops."[xxviii]

Monitoring and Protecting the Edge of the Enterprise

Organizations can also be more proactive on security, instead of simply patching and updating systems, and having anti-malware software installed, an organization can actively scan for viruses and malware on any content coming into the environment. This might be scanning incoming email messages and attachments, it might include having any USB thumb drive or device plugged into a system scanned before the device is made available to the operating system, or having any content transferred, downloaded, or accessed over the internet scanned.

Leveraging security tools and technologies and help identify and minimize the impact of security threats in the environment. The monitoring process also proactively looks for security threats, just like a building is more secure when a security officer walks the corridors of the building and the perimeter of the building periodically than simply waiting for a burglar alarm to go off.

Advancing the Roles and Responsibilities of Hosters and eCommerce Providers in Cyber Protection

Organizations that host data, applications, email systems, websites, virtual machines, or the like for others have an added responsibility for cyber-protections. Most hosting organizations wouldn't even get started in the business if they didn't have adequate documented security policies and processes in place as businesses would not trust the organization to host their applications and data. The key to a hosted provider is "trust". Users have to trust that the organization will protect their information. If that trust is lost, the organization will have customers leave the organization and not do business with it.

Trust is gained by having multiple layers of security that is well documented as well as a track record of maintaining a secured environment. The track record is hopefully developed over months / years of safe and secured operations. The security is multi-layered so that the hoster organization will have physical security that prevents users from physically accessing the network and data equipment without proper credentials, active logging and tracking, network security detection equipment, multi-layer software encryption, anti-malware, and other protections.

Protecting Data Collected as Part of the User's Access Process

Organizations collecting data such as logons, passwords, credit card information, and personally identifiable information need to take even extra care. With far too common accounts of credit card security violations occurring from attacks on department stores or online retailers, organizations need to have even better protection in place for ongoing security protection.

The chain of custody of protected information needs to be clearly isolated and made available only on a need to know basis. Organizations should be careful not to hold user information, credit card information, bank information, and personally identifiable information in common databases that a single attack can access all of the information at the same time.

Through security best practices on data management, organizations can maintain encrypted data, and separate key pieces of data so that it takes the compromise of multiple systems running on multiple platforms to access critical information. NIST provides general guidance on system server security as it relates to databases and other applications stored on servers in their guide 800-123, "Guide to General Server Security."[xxix]

It's also important for an organization to assume that it will be attacked and that basic security systems like firewalls and network segmentation will protect them. In an environment where firewalls and networks are not assumed to be secure, the organization takes even more care and control over the actual databases and data systems managing the information.

With practices to protect information with multiple processes of security, an organization can make it more difficult for information to be accessed through authorized means. NIST provides general guidance on information system security in their guide 800-14, "Generally Accepted Principles and Practices for Securing Information Technology Systems."[xxx]

Looking for Signs of Differences in Performance or Operations

In addition to traditional system monitoring and intrusion detection processes, organizations can put in place processes to monitor changes in performance and operations. As experienced with an incident of an open source bug known as Heartbleed where passwords were exposed, a couple organizations identified the bug before it was made more public. The organizations that identified the bug weren't looking for the bug or security violation itself, they were monitoring the operations of their systems. After a patch and update, they recognized that the systems were operating differently than before as it related to response time and communication systems processing. While the response was nominal, it was "different" than expected, and from that, the engineers went to work to identify specifically what was causing the timing and performance issues. They had stumbled across the Heartbleed bug weeks before anyone else knew about it.

It is this additional due diligence in knowing how systems operate, and the impact and effect of systems operations that makes one organization proactively aware of how their systems are operating and any potential security bug and violation, versus other organizations that wait until someone else finds a problem and reports on it. This is the difference of good security versus great security, as an organization waiting for a problem is already a step or two behind the cybercriminals. The organization that is proactive to problems can be a step or two AHEAD of the cybercriminals, and when it comes to customer trust, it is important to be ahead rather than behind the security of the bad guys.

THE ROLES AND RESPONSIBILITIES OF ENTERPRISES IN CYBER PROTECTION

8 PROTECTING AN ENVIRONMENT BY STARTING WITH RELEVANT I.T. SECURITY GOALS

A common question gets asked by organizations all the time, how much and what type of security should we have? The answer of course is "it depends", which it really does depend on what the organization is REQUIRED to have versus the level of security the organization like LIKE to have. The differences typically are between the levels of penalties imposed on the organization. If someone will go to jail (like a Chief Executive of the organization) then an organization has regulatory requirements (with penalties) that the organization will adhere to. However if the security is "nice to have" and the there are no active penalties or recourse to the organization or someone in management, then the requirement is typically deeded optional.

Confirming the Security you Must Have

For security that you "must have", regulatory laws always float to the top of the "must have" list. Things like the Health Insurance Portability and Accountability Act (HIPAA), Payment Card Industry (PCI) data security standard, Gramm-Leach-Bliley Act (GLBA), Sarbanes-Oxley Act (SOX), Food and Drug Administration 21CFR, and the like are regulations that can throw a Chief Executive into jail or potentially shut a business down, so organizations adhere to the requirements of these regulations quite stringently.

In most cases, these regulations dictate the level of security required, the length of time access needs to be managed, and the auditing and reporting requirements needed. Best practices are generated for what is typically required that organizations can follow the general rules and guidance. Many organizations go beyond the generally accepted guidance and create their own levels of security based on their interpretation of the regulations. The "right" amount of compliance to regulations depends on what the organization chooses as their best practices, whether they follow generally accepted guidance, or if they feel a more in-depth level is required. Either case, good documentation is always a best practice at ensuring security is addressed as needed.

Identifying Security You Should Have

After required security has been addressed, organizations can go another level to address security that they "should have". Many would say that this level of security is a requirement, and no doubt when we're talking about employee information privacy, customer confidentiality, or trade secrets, that level of information protection is usually of utmost importance to an organization. However unlike regulatory security requirements that can send a Chief Executive to jail or force an organization to go out of business because of a failure to comply with the law, protecting trade secrets and employee information is extremely important, but the penalties are at most fines, or will cause a public relations embarrassment for the organization, but no one typically goes to jail in these instances.

The difference in a "should have" security identifies the level of security and effort the organization places in protection this information. Many organizations hold certain trade secrets with the highest level of protection because if they lose the security of key information, the organization can lose its competitive advantage or by contract, the organization may be sued by a customer for the breech of secured information. However some trade secrets are openly shared by marketing departments to prove how special an organization is and how unique their business is. As an example, and organization that has a patent on a process might openly share the process because the process is protected by law, and also patents are a matter of public information, so it's not like the information is particularly "secret".

So organizations invest in security mechanisms relative to the cost of loss of the information, or relative to the legal liability that might result if the information is compromised. There are many laws these days that do take commonly stored data information and raise the level of security protection to an extremely high level. As an example, employee personnel information may be protected by HIPAA and thus what used to be just employee data is now protected by regulation. This is where it is important for an organization to keep track of laws and regulations, and clearly know whether something that once was classified as "should have security" is now deemed "must have security" for protection.

Addressing Security You Would Like to Have

Next on the rank of information protection is addressing security that an organization would "like to have" protected. In these cases, no one will go to jail for the failure to protect the information, and the organization likely won't get sued if the security is compromised. These "like to have" security are things such as employee vs contractor access to information, best practices at changing of passwords, keeping systems patched and up to date, protecting systems with multiple layers of security defense, and the like. These items are intended to provide security and protection to various components of the business and are typically deemed "best practices. For organizations that are seeking to be as secure as possible, it should go far beyond what is "required" and what it "should have" for security, and invest into many layers of security of things an organization "would like to have" to better strengthen security for the enterprise.

Applying People, Process, and Technology to Security Initiatives

Many frameworks address the triangle of people, process, and technology in addressing things within the I.T. industry, and as it relates to security initiatives, the triangle also directly applies. Many organizations go out and buy a "security device" or a series of software products and then believe they are "secure".

However, as has been addressed so far in this book, it's more than just technology that will solve security challenges. There's a huge need to ensure that employees are doing their part to be safe and aware, and there are policies and processes that can be applied to people's behavior as well as technology rules to proactively manage and reactively monitor security in the enterprise.

The solution in security is not to depend on a single factor, but to create layers of defense so that if there's a breach of one layer, there's another layer available to provide protections. It's key to ensuring that security is a combination of people, process, and technology in combination and in layers that'll help an organization thwart off a security attack.

Understanding the Business Culture and Tolerance for Security Enforcement

Cybersecurity is also one of those things that doesn't equally apply across any and all businesses the same. There have been highly successful security experts that move from one business to another that were very successful thwarting security threats in the prior environment that failed miserably in a new environment.

Being that security is more than a product or a policy, but also includes people to the equation, the success of security enforcement is influenced by the overall culture of the organization.

In highly regulated industries like bio-tech, healthcare, securities, or defense organizations that already have extensive policies for security standards, it is easier to enforce cybersecurity policies. When an employee has to physically sign in every morning, leave their mobile phones at the gate, enter in passcodes to get into their workspace, have 2 or 3 mechanisms to log into their system, are body scanned as they leave the facility to ensure the employee isn't leaving with data or devices, those environments already have a strong process for physical security that makes it easier to apply cybersecurity controls.

However for start-up organizations or non-tech focused organizations, the culture of open-ness or the lack of focus on security in general makes it harder if not extremely difficult to enforce restrictive policies on security. When the nature of the organization is to freely share ideas and information, putting encryption restrictions and multiple levels of security to share content goes against the culture of the business. This is where many start-ups that shift from a "seat of the pants" mode in incubation that then go public and have to comply by regulatory requirements of a publicly traded organization have challenges making the transition into highly structured and security minded environments.

Small businesses frequently find security enforcement costly and difficult to fund, so budget is key to those organizations in setting and applying security controls. While users might be open to protecting data, the cost of technology or the complexity of implementing policies and processes cause security control breakdowns in smaller organizations.

All of this is a cycle that requires the cooperation of individuals, with a top down management acceptance to security controls, with the proper technologies in place to automate security systems, with policies and processes that are setup to manage technology devices and provide guidance to employees on their roles and responsibilities to the security system.

9 DEVELOPING AN EFFECTIVE I.T. SECURITY STRATEGY

So how does an organization create an effective I.T. security strategy, and then successfully apply it to the organization? As has been shared so far in this text, it's more than just buying a device and plugging it in, and it's more than being heavy handed and dictate policies that employees have to follow. It's an entire process that builds goals, awareness, support, communications, adoption, and enforcement that makes a successful security strategy plan for an organization.

Understanding the Business Goals and Focus of a Business

The first thing organization do when addressing cybersecurity is define the security goals for the organization. This is one of the first challenges an organization has as it typically depends on a "security expert" to set the security goals for the organization. However when you step back and think about the motivation of the security expert, their security mind will put them into a mode of creating as tight of security and implementation of security best practices before even understanding the overall culture and nature of the business.

The security needs of a pre-school is different than the security needs of a government defense contract organization. The security needs of a non-profit community outreach organization is different than the security needs of a law firm.

Before jumping into the security goals of the organization, it is best to start with the business goals and business focus of the organization. The real basics of "what do you do" and "what do you need to protect" is a good start in creating a security framework for the organization. A pre-school will likely identify the physical protection of the children under their care as most important, and from a cybersecurity perspective the content that might be shared with the children from technology devices. Security can be used to monitor physical entrance and exit, photo identification system of parents and caretakers dropping off and picking up children. Filters and protection to prevent inappropriate information from being displayed on tablet and teaching devices will likely be of interest. And the childcare center likely has health records and personal contact information that needs to be protected, however very simple controls like having that information on a system that is not connected to the Internet can very simply minimize the need for complicated firewalls and intruder detection systems. Because once you take personal information off internet facing systems and keep that data separate, there's very little left in a childcare environment that requires more extensive cybersecurity other than content filters.

However for a defense contractor or manufacturer, trade secrets are crucial, and the protection of intellectual and protected property is highly important. However for these organizations, it's about the protection of content, so as long as the content is encrypted and protected from leakage outside of the organization, as well as conversations are protected and blocked from external transmission, a defense contractor can put walls up around what they need to protect, no different than putting barbed wire fencing and lookout posts around facilities of the past.

This is a different type of security than healthcare organizations where it's not about silo'd data that is being protected, but around the privacy of information. Healthcare organizations don't need to simply protect information, they need to ensure that data and communications is shared internally as well as with external individuals like patients and the patient's doctors. It's a whole different type of security protection model that is required since the senders and recipients of information may not be part of the healthcare organization, so external access is needed.

These and dozens of other scenarios clearly identify how cybersecurity is DIFFERENT for each and every organization, and a one size, one policy, best practice model does not apply. Organizations need to define "their business" and what they are trying to protect, and then apply appropriate security.

Translating Security Goals into Enforceable Security Strategy

In Chapter 8, we identified regulatory requirements that set the foundation of security that an organization "must have", this is a good place to start. By focusing on protecting regulated data, an organization can define what it needs to enforce. Important in this process is to target the regulated data and identify whether the organization really needs to apply stringent security across everything in the organization. Many organizations get so tied up around compliance security that they apply a one-size fits all approach so that every email, document, electronic form, or bit of data has the same level of security, which makes the entire organization bloated with policies and processes on systems that do not require enforcement.

For regulations around Sarbanes-Oxley as it relates to communications of the Chief Executive Officer, Chief Financial Officer, and Chief Operating Officer specific to communications and disclosure of business information, the protection of communications of these individuals need to be logged and kept for seven years, but the same level of storage of information of the other 95+% of information in the organization does not need to be retained for 7-years. And even for these executives, ONLY communications related to the financial and operational health of the business need to be retained. If the execs are planning to go grab lunch on Friday, or if the execs are talking about a football game over the weekend, that content does not need to be logged, tracked, and stored. Again, it's about applying the right policy to the right amount of information for the right individuals, and not keep everything for everyone about anything.

Applying the "must have", "should have", and "would like to have" policies as they relate to the goals of the organization in a manner that is targeted and makes sense sets the process in motion to security information for the enterprise.

Creating Consistent Policies and Standards for Enforcement

Another important focus for organization is to create security policies that are consistent with the goals of the organization. In many environments, an organization creates very restrictive policies on Microsoft Windows systems, but there are no policies and enforcement on data stored on mobile phones, Apple Mac systems, or other devices. If a policy is important enough to apply to one device, it should be important to apply to all instances of devices, systems, and access methods.

It's not about "securing everything across all devices", again, it's about targeting information that needs to be secured, but then if you are going to secure "that information", then be consistent in the application of security across any and all systems for that information.

Additionally, once it is identified what information needs to be protected, it is important to enforce the security of the information across all levels and ranks within the organization. Far too often organizations set policies that are less restrictive for the executives of the organization, so while everyone in the company has to change their passwords every 30-days, execs in the organization may only have to change their password every 6 months. You have to step back and ask what makes a password policy for execs any less restrictive than others in the organization. If it is good enough to have a 6 month password change policy for execs, then it is likely okay to have a 6 month password change policy for everyone in the organization. Or if there is an important reason to have a password change every 30-days, then it should apply to everyone, including the executives.

Similarly, if data is deemed important enough to be encrypted with passwords or some type of data leakage protection technology, then everyone accessing the information should have the encryption policy enforced. Executives should not be except from encrypted content, and quite frankly, most executives have access to highly sensitive information and data encryption is likely even more important for data being accessed by the executives. Consistent policies should be applied to all users, or the policy needs to be reviewed to determine whether the security policy is appropriate and what measures should be applied across the enterprise to ultimately address the overall security goals of the organization.

Identifying the Need for Top Down Management Communications

With the right focus and targeting of security on the right information, that is then applied consistently across the enterprise (including being adhered to by executives in the organization), the next step is to have a top down communications of the importance of security and overall adherence to the security policies.

Organizations that have a senior executive (preferably the President, CEO, or CFO) step up and share the importance of security and that security is adhered to from the top of the organization, the likelihood of the adherence of the policies is better archived. If the executives believe in the security policies and abide by the policies, then there is a better chance others will accept the policies and do their part in the people aspects of security enforcement.

This is also why it is important that security policies "make sense" and that executives aren't except from policies. Policies that make good sense and are targeted at key information are easy to follow as long as the goals and importance of adhering to the tighter security is shared across the organization.

Planning and Preparing for User Adoption

With business and security strategy goals in mind, along with executive management support, security policies and processes can be rolled out, however the key is to get user acceptance and adoption to actually get security practices to take hold.

A common practice is to create a training and communications program that shares with employees the importance of security in the organization, the due care taken in targeting security (not making it broadly generic across the entire organization), and making the security policies direct and relevant. An "All Hands" meetings that brings together all employees with direct involvement of senior management helps to share information as well as invoke questions and feedback. Doing something like an "All Hands" meeting that is not a normal process can get everyone's attention, so more than just an email blast or article buried in the company newsletter, but something that puts in focus the needs and requirements for a secured environment.

Prior to broad companywide communications might be to sample a handful of users with the new policies so that any common questions, issues, feedback, and the like can be teased out with a test group before going out to the entire company. The smaller test group could even try out the new policies, see how impactful (or not) the policies are, see whether the policies actually are easy to adhere to during the normal course of the day so that hopefully the impact is minimal on users, but the value to the organization in protecting information will be great.

Anticipate within the roll-out plan enough time for user adoption and understanding. When applying policies, many times there are variations to policy enforcement that differentiate between "require" or "recommend" policies so that for a 30-day period, higher restrictions are recommended and lightly implemented so that users can ease themselves into the tools and technologies (and their individual roles) in security, than to all of a sudden get forced into following detailed steps to do a simple task. Easing users into the security policies will help the organization adopt security hopefully in a smoother manner.

When enforcing security policies, there are two options, either yell at users for not following policies, or to openly help and share with users the policy and how they do their part in security execution. No one wants to be yelled at, and learning new processes can take time, especially for users that might not send emails or secured documents every day, it might be a couple weeks before someone comes across a situation where they need to send or access a protected document. So while the policy may have gone in effect "weeks ago", 2-3 weeks might pass before a user might be confronted with the new security process.

By making security support easy and friendly, it has been found that users are willing to ask questions, ask for help, actually do their part in security than to be afraid of the security policy, afraid to ask questions and "look stupid," and the employee then find ways "around" the security policy.

Overcoming Objections and Getting All Employees to Participate in the Security Plan

During the trial period or test period on security, users might ask the question "why" a policy is needed, and it is helpful to prepare good answers because if the response is "because", users won't understand and are less likely to actively participate in their role for the new security systems. Organizations want their users to accept security policies in a manner where the policy is important to the employee themselves, then they will be active participants and do their share to provide security and protection.

Security roll-outs also don't happen overnight. As much as the I.T. department likely has worked on the security planning and implementation process for weeks or months, for users, it is all new to them. And again, for those users who might only occasionally handle secured content, it might be another couple weeks or couple months before they are confronted with the new to do something about that new security policy "thing". An even when they participate in the new security process once, it might be weeks or months before they have to do something security related again. So the guidance and support to users is a long term process, and how they understand their role in supporting a secured environment is critical not only on day 1, but ongoing.

Getting Management Approval and Rolling Out a Comprehensive Security Plan

As has been shared previously, management approval and communications of the importance of security and their usage of the same security tools and processes is important from a top down perspective. But management's support is also not a one-time process, and ongoing management communications on security is very helpful. Having management write articles about security, the success the organization (hopefully) has had in making the environment more secure, hearing about the feelings of the management in their support of a more secured environment continues to keep the message clear throughout the organization.

Evolving Security Policies to Meet the Evolving Threats on Security

Cybersecurity is an ongoing process that changes over time. The minute you patch up one hole, the bad guys seem to find other holes to compromise, so security is an evolving process. That said, the implementation of new policies, new security methods becomes key. By making it clear early on that security policies are evolving and policies will change, it'll help ensure employees will continue to evolve their role in security as security threats change and systems and modified to address the changes.

Conversely, as security threats diminish, it is just as important to remove security policies and loosen up security, than always keeping them tight. Again, back to the relevance of policies, if an old policy no longer makes sense, it is helpful to remove the policy so that ALL policies make sense and users can accept adoption of the policy because it is relevant to their day to day work efforts.

Some may argue that once a security threat, always a security threat, which is true, one could just apply a blanket warning across any and all security vectors forever. But just like air travel where knives aboard airplanes in the United States were banned for a decade, the Transportation Security Administration (TSA) lifted the ban on knives not because knives somehow became "safe", but rather there are other vectors that are more dangerous. Rather than security officers looking for small knives that are really no more harmful than a ballpoint pen or a knitting needle that are allowed with no restrictions on airplanes, the TSA could spend their time looking for current security vectors like plastic explosives or chemical-based weapons.

Again, security vectors have evolved, and prioritizing security threats can ensure more focus on the most vulnerable areas of cybersecurity.

10 CREATING ENFORCEABLE I.T. SECURITY POLICIES

Security policies have varying levels of enforceability, where good policies are easier to enforce because of user acceptance and adoption of a good policy, and bad policies are hard to enforce because if users don't understand the policies, they are less likely to do their part in adhering to the policy.

Understanding Good and Bad Security Policies

When creating a security policy with the desire to create nothing but enforceable good policies, a good security policy is one that targets the specific security threat you are working to protect against. As an example, if you are trying to protect documents from leaving the organization that are specific to the development of new products the company has in development, then the policy should focus on the protection of content revolving around new product development.

If the goal is to prevent the release of credit card and private client information, then anything related to the collection, management, and storage of credit card and client information should be the focus of the organization's security priorities.

On the other hand, bad security policies are those that are not directly targeted at the security goals of the organization. Using the above examples, if the focus is around credit card and client information protection, but the organization requires two factor access to emails, unless credit card information and client information is exchanged over the email system, this two factor security policy does not align with the stated organizational goal. It's not to say that the organization might require two factor access to emails for other business purposes, but when the primary goal is to protect credit card information, then this resulting use of technology does not directly align with the business need, and as such is not a good justifiable policy and process.

Or in the case of content protection, if the organization is focused at protecting new product development information by encrypting all documents and development data, but then enforces a policy that requires the encryption of ALL information including simple emails or 1-page memos (not related to product development), then again, the policy does not directly match the business requirements.

The organization needs to list the business goals and security goals, and then prioritize the protection level for each item on the list. An organization that comes up with a list that is 15 items long, but the top 7 items are of most importance, the organization should ensure that the top 7 items are addressed, but could identify that the balance 8 on the list are not of importance. There comes that tipping point where having too much security hinders employees ability to do their job and can frustrate employees so that an organization that has strong support for the top 5 items is better off than an organization that tries to address 15 items, but employees are inconvenienced and choose to not address ANY of the items. Drawing a line in what to support and what to not support actually can improve security, than trying to address everything, but doing it poorly.

Importance of Usability in Security Enforcement

Complex security requirements can limit employee's access to critical information in a timely manner, and the balance of security versus employee's ability to get their job done becomes important for an organization.

Something organizations frequently find is that when an employee has too many security requirements that they don't understand or necessarily agree with, they will tend to "work around the system" which has touched off a growth of use of cloud-based storage systems like Box.com, or Dropbox, or the like where employees are forced to encrypt or protect content internally, so they just use an external service. These external services create a higher level of security threat to critical information for the organization than the organization had intended, as such, a focus on targeted priorities is key.

A Single Workaround can Thwart the Entire Security Effectiveness for an Enterprise

Policies that restrict users from doing their jobs that the users do not understand or see the purpose of will commonly be ignored. As noted in the last section, users will find workarounds to get their job done, or do what they think is more efficient use of their time. A single workaround can thwart the entire efforts of the organization in having a secure environment. As seen case after case, a disgruntled government contractor can steal enough confidential government documents that can do lasting harm to the U.S. government for many years to come. Or a single hole in security for a retail giant can create a backdoor access to tens of millions of credit card and shopper personal information.

It only takes one hole, one employee, one weak link to undo the cybersecurity of an entire organization. So the effectiveness of security is not to try to lock everything down, but to lock down the most important areas and ensure the protection of those areas is ensured.

Nesting and Combining Various Policies to Meet Different Needs of the Organization

There are various ways policies can be created and applied to users and systems, with the most commonly seen, but not necessarily the best method, which is to have a standard policy for everyone (i.e.: password policy) and then dozens of individual policies. This works great for the first dozen or so policies, but once new policies are added, then new policies, and then more new policies, there are hundreds if not thousands of policies, and it's hard to sift through what policy applies to whom, or why.

A more practical approach to creating policies is to layer policies based on the organizational needs. If a policy applies to everyone, then it might be an O-, organizational policy. If a policy applies to everyone in a specific site, then a policy might be an S-, site policy. Policies that apply to users of specific departments might get a D- policy or an R- role policy.

By creating a hierarchy of policies and then nesting the policies, an organization can more easily see what policies are applied, and why. If a site is collapsed, the policy either needs to be collapsed and removed, or a new policy implemented. Or if a policy only applies to members of the financial department, then it's clear that the policy only applies to members of a specific department.

From a policy review and audit standpoint, an organization can determine if an organization wide policy is still even applicable to everyone in the organization, or whether a departmental policy is appropriate anymore. Again, part of the structure is to not only add policies as needed, but to be able to remove policies that are no longer applicable.

Assessing and Evaluating Policies to Confirm they Consistently Meet the Needs of the Organization

Security policies should be regularly reviewed to determine if the policies are still applicable. Best practices can be assessed from time to time to determine what are the most common policies that are being implemented, and how those best practices apply to the specific organization.

It's always a good idea to annotate policies so that it is clear months or years down the line why a policy was created in the first place. Many times, years pass and someone inherits the security management of an organization, but there is no documentation noting why the organization has the security policies it has. And years later, many times users or the management don't remember why either.

However, rather than just ignoring policies and leave them as is, documentation would be of best help identifying the purpose, goal, and intent of a policy, or all else fails if a reason cannot be determined, the policy should be immediately removed.

Policies should be crystal clear to management and employees, and if the policy can't be justified, it's a good reason to have the policy eliminated.

Another good practice is that every time a new policy is added, that an old policy should be sought out and eliminated. While this doesn't always work as additive policies are important, and removing a policy for the sake of just removing a policy is also not a good practice, at least considering the removal of a policy can force the organization to "think" about each and every policy in place.

This constant are regular attention to cleaning up policies, as well as a good practice of documenting policies and their purpose helps an organization maintain a consistent environment with clear goals and manageable security expectations.

11 LEVERAGING EFFECTIVE SOLUTIONS TO SIMPLIFY POLICY ENFORCEMENT

With business and security goals in mind, and a practice of creating, implementing, and managing policies in general, now to get in to specific policies that can be implemented to create effective results with simple policies.

Focusing on Basic Patterns of Security Can Aid in Simplifying Security Demands

Technologies can restrict access and usability as well as technologies can aid and assist employees in security enforcement. The important part of this is to ensure that the solutions implemented into an environment are more of the latter than of the former, where technologies themselves aid in security enforcement.

Automation is a good solution for this, instead of having employees "add" more clicks and steps to their day to day tasks, if there's an automated process that can be implemented to scan and address security, then that'll take the user out of the path and ease in the implementation of a security environment. As an example, no one spends an extensive amount of their day dealing with anti-malware software for email messages. In this day and age, emails go through filters that capture 95-98% of the incoming spam. At times it might not seem like the anti-spam filters are good enough at catching spam, however there's a ton more spam email messages coming through to you than you are actually getting thanks for anti-malware tools commonly in place in organizations and public mail systems.

Because the automated systems trap the worst offenders of email spam, a user only needs to address a handful of messages. What if instead of getting 3-4 spam messages, you had 30-40 (or 300-400) spam messages to deal with? That would add time to your day to sift through that many junk messages. Similarly, automation tools can be used to automatically encrypt content or decrypt content, making it seamless to users to protect information, but not have to actually "do" something special.

Performing Content Classification to Aid Policy Enforcement

Rather than encrypting everything, a common method of protecting content is to classify the content. In content classification, keywords are searched that meet specific criteria such as the word "confidential" or a document with the phrase "top secret project x" or the like. A lexicon can be created by the organization that seeks out specific words, or potentially a combination of works, so that it requires 2 or 3 hits before a document is classified, such as a document that has the word confidential along with the phrase "top secret project x". Classification systems come in varying forms with the ability to identify words that are near others, so the word classification that is near the phrase "top secret project x" might be identified for categorization.

Additionally, classification can be applied only to documents that might be going from one employee to another, as an example, an organization might be focused on just content going between the CEO, CFO, and COO to apply SOX-based security policies. Or an organization might want to just search content from the financial and the human resource department, to look for content that might be deemed confidential or protected.

For organizations looking to protect intellectual property coming out of the engineering department, the organization can look to classify just documents going to and from that department with keywords that might be specific to that department.

There are a LOT of variations, end of the day, the organization can do content classification to aid in the implementation and enforcement of certain security policies.

Once content is classified, the organization can then look to apply policies, so content that might be flagged as protected that is coming from the engineering department or to and from the finance department or to and from managers might now be tagged for encryption. However the same tagged document that is heading out to a public internet address might be blocked for transmission. This allows an organization to take content classified content, and apply a policy based on where the document or content is headed.

Protecting Content Instead of Hardening the Exterior

A big movement in cybersecurity is to move away from hardening the exterior of an enterprise with firewalls and complex network security systems that create a strong outer shell to the organization, and instead focus on the protection of data itself. As has been seen many times in the past, an organization can harden their network so that intruders can't get into the network, but then a disgruntled employee simply loads up a thumb drive or laptop with a lot of sensitive company information and walks out the front door. For many organizations, security does not always come from an external intruder, the problem is frequently internally focused.

By encrypting sensitive data and enforcing a policy that users have to logon to access the data, this sets in motion security on what is deemed critical to the organization which is their data. The logon credentials to access data can be tied to an employee's network logon account. If the employee is terminated, their logon credentials are disabled, and thus the user no longer has access to the data that might be sitting on their laptop or thumb drive.

This encryption of content also prevents the "leakage" of information as users upload content to public sites like Dropbox, Box.com, or OneDrive to share the content with others, but then lose track of who they are sharing what information to. Over time entire folders are freely accessible, but the user forgets and copies up content that should not be shared to others. With encrypted content that requires a logon credential to access the information, even if content is left in a publicly accessible folder, the only way to open the content is to enter in an authorized credential.

These logon credentials are typically tied to the Active Directory logon managed by the enterprise that users log in to every day. However there are external directories that provide logon credentials to external users as well. It could be tagged to something like a Windows LiveID type account, or it could be tied to an Azure Active Directory cloud-based account, or some other trusted logon authority.

That way users within an organization as well as users outside an organization can share content with logon credentials, and the content can be tagged to allow or block access, as well as content can be tagged to automatically expire for access after a certain period of time.

Utilizing Automation to Aid Security Enforcement

We've already addressed automation in terms of the automatic scanning of email messages for anti-malware access, however with a combination of content classification with something like rights management encryption protection of content that ties content access to logon credentials, an organization can automate the encryption of information.

This automated encryption can be set on email systems that filter incoming and outgoing email messages so that information leaving the organization and going to an external email address could be automatically encrypted in transit. Or content that is stored in a shared repository like Microsoft SharePoint, or stored in a Microsoft OneDrive for Business account can have encryption policies automatically applied when the content is saved that'll encrypt the content on save.

Enforcement is best when employees don't have to "think" or "do things", that security protection is automatically done for them. And with logical policies, content can be analyzed and associated with specific policies, tagged with classification information, and then encrypted when a specific trigger like the content is being emailed outside the organization, or being saved outside the organization that the content is duly encrypted and protected.

Encrypting Content in Transit and Content at Rest

The process where content is encrypted as it is saved to a file system or is encrypted as it is transmitted over email is called "Encrypting Content in Transit". This is done for content that is moving through the enterprise.

However, many times content already exists on fileservers, SharePoint servers, sitting as emails in Exchange, that content is not moving anywhere, or is said to be "at rest". The ability to classify, encrypt, and protect that content is just as important as managing the content in transit, so the technology that takes content both in transit and at rest, and protects that content is an important solution for data protection for an enterprise.

Monitoring Points of Data Access and Egress to Assess Information Flow and Policy Enforcement Effectiveness

The question comes up, what happens to information that might not be on a managed fileserver, email system, SharePoint system, or the like that can classify content and protect it in transit, such as content that might reside on a user's home laptop that they bring into the office and start to upload or download content. In those cases, there are tools that monitor the data access and egress points of the network, effectively monitoring traffic that goes in and out of firewalls. The same type of filter and rule can be placed on the firewalls to look for content and then apply a classification on the content and encrypt the content in transit.

There are companies like Sky High Networks[xxxi] in Cupertino, California that have a cloud-based service that monitors network access to cloud service points. Users that might be uploading content to Box.com, Dropbox, Google, Instagram, OneDrive, or the like can be filtered and a report generated for the organization. The organization can block egress to sites not authorized by the organization, or it can enable filters and content encryption on targeted information. Lots of options by simply listening for targets and enabling policies to be applied as appropriate.

LEVERAGING EFFECTIVE SOLUTIONS TO SIMPLIFY POLICY ENFORCEMENT

12 PREPARING FOR THE FUTURE

As we wrap up this book, we look to prepare ourselves for the future in a world where cybersecurity threats continue to expand, and as soon as we think we have appropriate protections in place, another threat comes along.

Security Risks are Always Evolving

One thing to be certain about security risks is that they will always evolve and something new will always pop up. To keep up with security threats, organizations need to be proactive and assess the current state of risks as they relate to the organization's security protection systems and processes in place. A scan of best practices is always helpful to see where the organization fits in to addressing ongoing threats, or whether new best practices might suggest changes in how the organization addresses security threats.

Additionally, keeping up on trade information, conference materials, and security standards can help an organization ensure it has the latest information available. Hardware and software vendors publish their own security guides and provide guidance on security protections. It is presumed that since security risks are evolving, that any information you get on security should be current information, within the past year as you can assume anything older than a year will already be part of your security plan and you're trying to be proactive and forward thinking.

Prepare to Be Responsive

As much as an organization does its best to be proactive in addressing security challenges, things come up and even the best managed security conscious organization will find itself in the middle of a security compromise situation.

When something comes up, the organization needs to be reactive, and respond as quickly as possible. This means monitoring the environment internally as well as externally, and determine if there are things that can be done or need to be done to address current threats.

When a security incident occurs, many times the incident happens to multiple organizations at the same time, from which best practices or guidance may be available to help the organization address the security event in real time with shared knowledge and experiences from others.

The key is to respond quickly, to minimize the footprint of any damage that might arise, yet be methodical in the approach, not rush out and buy a bunch of hardware and software, and completely redo years of policies and practices, but to quickly address the immediate threat, but take time to think through the longer term strategy and future proofing of the security of the organization.

New Risks are Added; Existing Risks are De-emphasized

As mentioned in Chapter 8 about focusing on current risks, and eliminating security policies that are not as crucial or as high of risk, this is where the evaluation of new and old risks are conducted. Instead of continuing to add protections to the organization making security a huge bundle of additive policies, as new and current risks are addressed, evaluate policies and the risks those policies have addressed, and eliminate or minimize security processes on the old stuff, so more time and effort can be spent on the new stuff.

Constantly create a priority list of risks, policies, and processes and rank them in order of importance. Focus on the top 5 or 10 items, and determine how much further down the list the organization needs to spend its time and energy addressing.

Get Confirmation From Management of Applicable Security Culture

The culture of the business was also addressed in Chapter 8, where start up organizations or organizations where the free flow of information and information sharing is key to the culture of the organization may have a harder time adopting stringent security policies. However organizations go through evolutions, so while an organization may have been against security policies early on in its lifecycle, as the organization matures, as the organization prepares to go public, as the organization has intellectual property that is important for it to protect, the attitudes on security change.

When the culture of the organization changes to more openly support security, while the company "has never had extensive security in the past," it may be more open to better information and privacy protection. Conduct culture assessments of the organization every 2-3 years, and gain buy-in from management when security requirements may be required due to a change in business status (i.e.: publicly traded, drugs going to clinical trial, patent protection is the basis of the organization's strategic advantage, etc.)

Ensure that management is willing to accept some level of risk to make day to day operations more responsive to employee needs, communicating the tradeoffs, communicating the risks, evolving organizational security strategies to meet the "current" business environment.

PREPARING FOR THE FUTURE

ABOUT THE AUTHOR

Rand Morimoto, Ph.D., MBA, CISSP, MCITP: Dr Morimoto was one of twelve Y2K Advisors to President Clinton, and the Cybersecurity Advisor to President Bush, leading the United States in Internet and compliance security policies and strategy. Dr Morimoto has a unique blend of deep technical knowledge and expertise, and an academic background in organizational behavior and organizational management.
Dr Morimoto is invited to speak at conferences and conventions around the world every year, and openly shares his knowledge and provides best practice guidance to government agencies, institutions, and enterprises of all sizes around the globe.
Dr Morimoto blends the psychology of cyberspace from his expertise in organizational behavior and organizational management with his deep rooted technical knowledge to develop best practices that help individuals and organizations remain cyber aware and cyber safe!

ENDNOTES

[i] New York Times, *In Hours, Thieves Took $45 Million in A.T.M. Scheme*, http://www.nytimes.com/2013/05/10/nyregion/eight-charged-in-45-million-global-cyber-bank-thefts.html?pagewanted=all&_r=0 (July 19, 2014).

[ii] Property Casualty 360, *Freight Increasingly at Risk for Cyber Crime*, http://www.propertycasualty360.com/2014/07/09/freight-increasingly-at-risk-for-cyber-crime (July 19, 2014).

[iii] Norton by Symantec, *Bots and Cybercrimes*, http://us.norton.com/cybercrime-botscybercrime (July 19, 2014).

[iv] Norton by Symantec, *What is Cybercrime?*, http://securityresponse.symantec.com/norton/cybercrime/definition.jsp (July 19, 2014).

[v] John R. Vacca and K Rudolph, *System Forensics, Investigation, and Response* (Sudbury, MA: Jones & Bartlett Learning, 2010), 27.

[vi] BBC News, *Writer Claims Viruses Were Harmless*, http://news.bbc.co.uk/2/hi/uk_news/wales/2680419.stm (July 19, 2014).

[vii] BBC News, *Love Bug Suspect Speaks*, http://news.bbc.co.uk/2/hi/science/nature/817269.stm (July 19, 2014).

[viii] Washington Post, *Paris Hilton Hack Started With Old Fashion Con*, http://www.washingtonpost.com/wp-dyn/content/article/2005/05/19/AR2005051900711.html (July 19, 2014).

[ix] Princeton University, *Script Kiddie* https://www.princeton.edu/~achaney/tmve/wiki100k/docs/Script_kiddie.html (July 19, 2014).

[x] The Register, *Parsons Not the Dumbest Virus Writer Ever*, http://www.theregister.co.uk/2003/09/01/parson_not_dumbest_virus_writer/ (July 19, 2014).

[xi] Microsoft Support, *Frequently Asked Questions About Word Macro Viruses*, http://support.microsoft.com/kb/187243 (July 19, 2014).

[xii] Microsoft Security Tech Center, *Microsoft Security Bulletin Advance Notification*, http://technet.microsoft.com/en-us/security/gg309152.aspx (July 19, 2014)

[xiii] How Stuff Works, *Why Would Daylight Savings Time Mess Up My Computer?*, http://computer.howstuffworks.com/dst-bug.htm (July 19, 2014).

[xiv] Out-Law.com, *Bank Hit by "Biggest Ever" Hack,* http://www.out-law.com/page-7679 (July 19, 2014).

[xv] eWeek Magazine, *Pump-and-Dump Hackers Gets 2 Years*, http://www.eweek.com/c/a/Security/Pump-and-Dump-Hacker-Gets-2-Years/ (July 19, 2014).

[xvi] U.S. Securities and Exchange Commission, *SEC v. Oleksandr Dorozkho, Civil Action No. 07 Civ. 9606,* http://www.sec.gov/litigation/litreleases/2010/lr21465.htm (July 19, 2014).

[xvii] Tech Republic, *What Makes Cybercrime Law So Difficult to Enforce,* http://www.techrepublic.com/blog/it-security/what-makes-cybercrime-laws-so-difficult-to-enforce/ (July 19, 2014).

[xviii] First Biz, *70% Decline in Security Vulnerabilities; but Deceptive Tactics More than Tripled,* http://firstbiz.firstpost.com/biztech/cybercriminals-giving-70-decline-security-vulnerabilities-deceptive-tactics-tripled-84225.html (July 19, 2014).

[xix] Federal Bureau of Investigation, *Combining Forces to Fight Cyber Crime,* http://www.fbi.gov/news/stories/2011/september/cyber_091611 (July 19, 2014).

[xx] Reid Skibell, "Cybercrimes & Misdemeanors: A Reevaluation of the Computer Fraud and Abuse Act" (Berkeley: University of California Berkeley, School of Law, 2003), 1-36.

[xxi] San Jose Mercury News, *California's Newest Cybercrime Task Force Unveiled in San Jose,* http://www.mercurynews.com/ci_19538586 (July 19, 2014).

[xxii] Federal Bureau of Investigation, *National Cyber Investigative Joint Task Force,* http://www.fbi.gov/about-us/investigate/cyber/ncijtf (July 19, 2014).

[xxiii] Martin E. Ford, "Motivating Humans: Goals, Emotions, and Personal Agency Beliefs" (Thousand Oaks: Sage Publishing, 1992), 202-238.

[xxiv] Business News Daily, *Email Scam Targets Executives: How to Protect Yourself,* http://www.businessnewsdaily.com/6410-corporate-executives-targeted-in-new-email-scam.html (July 19, 2014).

[xxv] Security Magazine, *Information Security – Top Down*, http://www.securitymagazine.com/articles/information-security-top-down-1 (July 19, 2014).

[xxvi] University of California, Berkeley, *Helping Workers Acquire Skills*, http://www.cnr.berkeley.edu/ucce50/ag-labor/7labor/05.htm (July 19, 2014).

[xxvii] U.S. Department of Commerce, *Guide to Intrusion Detection and Prevention Systems*, http://csrc.nist.gov/publications/drafts/800-94-rev1/draft_sp800-94-rev1.pdf (June 19, 2014).

[xxviii] U.S. Department of Commerce, *Guide to Malware Incident Prevention and Handling for Desktops and Laptops*, http://nvlpubs.nist.gov/nistpubs/SpecialPublications/NIST.SP.800-83r1.pdf (June 19, 2014).

[xxix] U.S. Department of Commerce, *Guide to General Sever Security*, http://csrc.nist.gov/publications/nistpubs/800-123/SP800-123.pdf (June 19, 2014).

[xxx] U.S. Department of Commerce, *Generally Accepted Principles and Practices for Securing Information Technology Systems*, http://csrc.nist.gov/publications/nistpubs/800-14/800-14.pdf (June 19, 2014).

[xxxi] Sky High Networks, http://www.skyhighnetworks.com/ (July 19, 2014).

www.ingramcontent.com/pod-product-compliance
Lightning Source LLC
Chambersburg PA
CBHW061032050326
40689CB00012B/2772

* 9 781500 583668 *